*GREATER THAN A [
AVAILABLE IN E

Greater Than a Tourist Book Series
Reviews from Readers

I think the series is wonderful and beneficial for tourists to get information before visiting the city.

-Seckin Zumbul, Izmir Turkey

I am a world traveler who has read many trip guides but this one really made a difference for me. I would call it a heartfelt creation of a local guide expert instead of just a guide.

-Susy, Isla Holbox, Mexico

New to the area like me, this is a must have!

-Joe, Bloomington, USA

This is a good series that gets down to it when looking for things to do at your destination without having to read a novel for just a few ideas.

-Rachel, Monterey, USA

Good information to have to plan my trip to this destination.

-Pennie Farrell, Mexico

Great ideas for a port day.
-Mary Martin USA

Aptly titled, you won't just be a tourist after reading this book. You'll be greater than a tourist!
-Alan Warner, Grand Rapids, USA

Even though I only have three days to spend in San Miguel in an upcoming visit, I will use the author's suggestions to guide some of my time there. An easy read - with chapters named to guide me in directions I want to go.
-Robert Catapano, USA

Great insights from a local perspective! Useful information and a very good value!
-Sarah, USA

This series provides an in-depth experience through the eyes of a local. Reading these series will help you to travel the city in with confidence and it'll make your journey a unique one.
-Andrew Teoh, Ipoh, Malaysia

>TOURIST

GREATER THAN A TOURIST- KISSIMMEE FLORIDA USA

50 Travel Tips from a Local

E.J. Robison

Greater Than a Tourist-Kissimmee Florida USA Copyright © 2019 by CZYK Publishing LLC. All Rights Reserved.

All rights reserved. No part of this book may be reproduced in any form or by any electronic or mechanical means including information storage and retrieval systems, without permission in writing from the author. The only exception is by a reviewer, who may quote short excerpts in a review.

The statements in this book are of the authors and may not be the views of CZYK Publishing or Greater Than a Tourist.

Cover designed by: Ivana Stamenkovic
Cover Image: https://pixabay.com/photos/lighthouse-sunrise-trees-palm-trees-3904303/

CZYK Publishing Since 2011.

Greater Than a Tourist

Lock Haven, PA
All rights reserved.

ISBN: 9781706415046

ND

>TOURIST
50 TRAVEL TIPS FROM A LOCAL

BOOK DESCRIPTION

Are you excited about planning your next trip? Do you want to try something new? Would you like some guidance from a local? If you answered yes to any of these questions, then this Greater Than a Tourist book is for you. Greater Than a Tourist- Kissimmee, Florida, United States by E.J. Robison offers the inside scoop on one of the most populated tourist cities in the entire world—from Disney World, the best snacks around, tours of the Everglades, and so much more! Most travel books tell you how to travel like a tourist. Although there is nothing wrong with that, as part of the Greater Than a Tourist series, this book will give you travel tips from someone who has lived at your next travel destination.

In these pages, you will discover advice that will help you throughout your stay. This book will not tell you exact addresses or store hours but instead will give you excitement and knowledge from a local that you may not find in other smaller print travel books.

Travel like a local. Slow down, stay in one place, and get to know the people and culture. By the time you finish this book, you will be eager and prepared to travel to your next destination.

Inside this travel guide book you will find:

- Insider tips from a local.
- Packing and planning list.
- List of travel questions to ask yourself or others while traveling.
- A place to write your travel bucket list.

OUR STORY

Traveling is a passion of the Greater than a Tourist book series creator. Lisa studied abroad in college, and for their honeymoon Lisa and her husband toured Europe. During her travels to Malta, an older man tried to give her some advice based on his own experience living on the island since he was a young boy. She was not sure if she should talk to the stranger but was interested in his advice. When traveling to some places she was wary to talk to locals because she was afraid that they weren't being genuine. Through her travels, Lisa learned how much locals had to share with tourists. Lisa created the Greater Than a Tourist book series to help connect people with locals. A topic that locals are very passionate about sharing.

TABLE OF CONTENTS

BOOK DESCRIPTION

OUR STORY

TABLE OF CONTENTS

DEDICATION

ABOUT THE AUTHOR

HOW TO USE THIS BOOK

FROM THE PUBLISHER

WELCOME TO

> TOURIST

Planning and Packing

1. Best Times to Visit

2. Where to Stay?

3. Do Your Research

4. What to Pack?

5. What to Buy When You Get Here

Money

6. Ways to Pay

7. Cash

8. Tips: Who Takes Them, Who Doesn't?

9. Be Prepared to Pay Extra

10. Banks and ATMs

11. Getting Around

12. From the Airport to the Hotel

13. Highways and Traffic

14. Tolls
15. Party of One

Food

16. Food for All Tastes!
17. Breakfast/Brunch
18. Quick Bites
19. Dinner
20. Farmer's Markets

Drinks and Snacks

21. Coffee
22. Tea
23. Famous Snacks
24. Bakeries
25. Coca-Cola Store
26. Malls
27. Disney Springs
28. Celebration
29. Tourist Shops
30. Grocery Stores/Supermarkets

Disney

31. Planning a Disney Vacation
32. Get the App!
33. Disney Resorts
34. Must-Sees and Must-Dos
35. Besides the Parks…

Other Attractions

36. Beaches
37. Other Major Theme Parks
38. Nature
39. Concerts
40. Waterparks
Unique Experiences
41. Escape Rooms
42. Silver Moon Drive-In Theater
43. Disney Wilderness Nature Preserve
44. Old Town
45. Downtown Kissimmee
Get Cultured
46. The Language
47. We're Never Strangers for Long!
48. Be Kind!
49. Art and Music
50. Please Recycle and Clean Up!
51. Explore!
TOP REASONS TO BOOK THIS TRIP
Other Resources:
Packing and Planning Tips
Travel Questions
Travel Bucket List
NOTES

DEDICATION

This book is dedicated to my Mama, who has always believed in me and shared my dreams. Kissimmee is her home too, and I hope I'm doing it justice.

ABOUT THE AUTHOR

E.J. Robison is an author and music teacher who lives in Kissimmee, FL. When not writing at Starbucks, you can find Elisabeth exploring Disney World, teaching music lessons, or reading a nice long book. Otherwise, she's off fulfilling her dream of traveling the world.

HOW TO USE THIS BOOK

The *Greater Than a Tourist* book series was written by someone who has lived in an area for over three months. The goal of this book is to help travelers either dream or experience different locations by providing opinions from a local. The author has made suggestions based on their own experiences. Please check before traveling to the area in case the suggested places are unavailable.

Travel Advisories: As a first step in planning any trip abroad, check the Travel Advisories for your intended destination.
https://travel.state.gov/content/travel/en/traveladvisories/traveladvisories.html

FROM THE PUBLISHER

Traveling can be one of the most important parts of a person's life. The anticipation and memories that you have are some of the best. As a publisher of the Greater Than a Tourist, as well as the popular *50 Things to Know* book series, we strive to help you learn about new places, spark your imagination, and inspire you. Wherever you are and whatever you do I wish you safe, fun, and inspiring travel.

Lisa Rusczyk Ed. D.
CZYK Publishing

>TOURIST

WELCOME TO
> TOURIST

>TOURIST

"You can't just read the guide book; you've got to throw yourself in! Eat the food, use the wrong verbs, get charged double, and end up kissing complete strangers. Or is that just me? Stop asking questions. Go and do it!"

-Doctor Who

When most people hear "Florida," they think of Orlando and Disney World. Few people know that the world-famous theme park is actually located in Kissimmee, a bustling city on the borderline between two huge counties. While the city is famous for its booming tourism business, Kissimmee is home to diverse cultures and people who know how to live life to the fullest. With this book, I invite you to live like that too, no matter how long your visit is!

When I first moved to Kissimmee, I just had constant thoughts of "wow." Though I moved here for a job, I stayed because I love the city. There is something to surprise you here every single day if you take the time to explore. And there's diversity here like there is nowhere else in the world; people who are here for only a week and live in a different country share their stories with people who have lived here their whole lives. This book is only a small part of my story living in Kissimmee, but I hope that it will help you when you visit one of the best cities in the world!

Bonus Pre-Tip: Talk Like a Kissimmee Resident

All across the world, we oftentimes take phrases we use in everyday conversation for granted. In Kissimmee, where there are so many popular places to reference, we often shorten the titles of theme parks, roads, and other things we come into contact with in daily life; just like you do wherever you live! Some of these I'll explain more in depth later, but they're important to understand as you read. So before you get started, here are some terms to know:

- Parks: unless I make it very clear I'm talking about an ordinary outdoor park, this word almost always refers to the popular theme parks nearby (Disney, Universal, SeaWorld, etc.).
- Celebration: An area that's kind of its own city, but still located inside Kissimmee
- 192: The main road that runs through Kissimmee.

>TOURIST

- 417 and 429: Toll roads that will take you North.
- I-4/Interstate 4: The major highway in Central Florida.

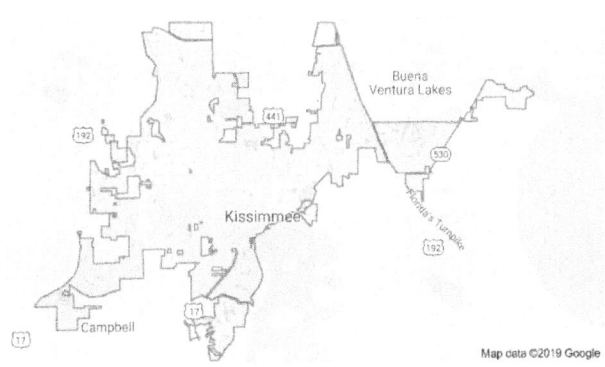

Kissimmee
Florida, USA

Kissimmee Climate

	High	Low
January	73	49
February	75	51
March	79	55
April	83	59
May	88	65
June	91	71
July	92	73
August	92	73
September	90	72
October	85	65
November	79	57
December	75	52

GreaterThanaTourist.com

Temperatures are in Fahrenheit degrees.
Source: NOAA

>TOURIST

PLANNING AND PACKING

1. BEST TIMES TO VISIT

The first thing you'll need to figure out when planning a trip to Kissimmee is when you're going to come. While much of that will involve working around your family's schedules, there are a few things to note about Kissimmee when deciding what time of year to visit.

A big factor to consider is the weather. June 1st through November 3rd is hurricane season in Florida, which means that conditions are favorable for hurricanes. However, if this part of the year works out best for you and your family, don't panic! Florida does not have a hurricane every year; in fact, quite often several years pass without a hurricane coming through.

You also need to be aware of the heat. Florida isn't called the "Sunshine State" for nothing! And with Kissimmee right in the middle of Central Florida, it gets the full power of the sunshine without an ocean breeze. February-April often has mild weather, around the 70s or 80s. May-September is really when Kissimmee gets the full summer heat, and days can range from 80-100+ degrees, with July and August being the hottest months of the year. October-December is relatively cooler, but not every day; we often experience 80-degree weather in December! However, by October, the summer weather will start to ebb away.

Summer is also the hottest time in Kissimmee as far as tourism goes. Summer days see the theme parks packed with people, and traffic on the highways at a standstill during rush hour. Therefore, if you're looking to beat the crowds, consider visiting Kissimmee in the winter or spring months (apart from April, during Spring Break time).

Think about planning your vacation around a certain event! There are concerts, festivals, and all sorts of different events happening throughout the year in Kissimmee. Maybe you can visit in the summer to attend a jazz festival, or in the fall to experience Epcot's world-famous Food and Wine Festival. Catching a special event is a great way to enjoy your vacation here!

>TOURIST

2. WHERE TO STAY?

One of the benefits of Kissimmee being such a renowned tourist destination is that there are lots of choices when it comes to where to stay. Because of the sheer abundance of people in the area and the traffic that can plague you at certain times of day, it's best to find a place that's close to where you'll be spending the most time. If you're heading to Disney World there are plenty of hotels on their property, but there are also lots of other motels and hotels very close by. No matter what your price range is, there's a place for you here!

Also, consider looking into Airbnb. While this option is sometimes overlooked, I've found as I've traveled that Airbnb has some of the best deals available, especially if you're looking to save money but still get great value. Many times you will often find a host who is willing to give you more information about the area as well!

3. DO YOUR RESEARCH

You've already started this step by picking up this book! There are tons and tons and tons of things to do in and around Kissimmee, so it's a good idea to have a look at all the available activities, even if you already have an idea of what you want your vacation to look like! Talk to your traveling companions and come up with a list of things you want to do in order of importance. Don't be afraid to do something new! Even if nature is the furthest thing from your mind when planning this trip, you might find yourself wanting to explore the Everglades while you're here or experience the unique and abundant wildlife in Florida!

If you're coming here just to visit the theme parks, that's great! However, I will say that lots of people come to Kissimmee, go to the theme parks, and never get to experience anything of the city outside of Disney or Universal. I love the parks, but even I'll admit that they can be exhausting! Think about planning some relaxing days of exploring the area and resting in between theme park days. Not only will it give you a break from long lines and being on your feet all day, but you'll also have a chance to experience all the other wonders Kissimmee has to offer!

A great resource to use is Trip Advisor. This website will show you everything there is to do in the area and give you reviews, prices, menus, etc. Another is the site Experience Kissimmee, which can give you details on anything and everything there is to do in Kissimmee. This website helped me to find some of my now go-to places when first moved here! They also have a blog that is worth a read, with articles like "Fall 2019 Foodie's Guide to Kissimmee" and "Star Wars: Galaxy's Edge Preview." The Visit Florida website can also give you more info on Kissimmee, including the average temperatures for each month of the year, nearest airports, and popular nearby cities.

4. WHAT TO PACK?

Bring things to wear that are comfortable and cool. Good shoes are also an absolute must when being out all day in Kissimmee! The sunshine is really bright here most of the time, so you'll thank yourself for bringing sunglasses or a hat to protect your eyes. Don't forget your bathing suit; with all the pools, waterparks, and beaches around, you'll most likely be in the water at some point during your stay!

If you're coming to Florida in the summer, you will experience lots of rain! Storms in Kissimmee can appear out of nowhere, even when the sun is out! It's essential to have an umbrella and a good rain jacket, as well as rubber boots or water-resistant shoes if you have them.

Make sure to bring a backpack or some kind of bag that's easy to carry all day! If you're hitting up the theme parks, you'll definitely need a backpack of some kind to carry everything in that won't be uncomfortable by the end of a long day.

Consider packing a reusable water bottle. With the heat in Kissimmee you'll need to drink a lot of water to stay hydrated, and bringing your own refillable bottle saves on money and helps the environment!

5. WHAT TO BUY WHEN YOU GET HERE

There are lots of essential items all Floridians need, even if you're only going to be a Floridian for a week or two. However, some things are better to buy when you get here because they're hard to find in other places or just a hassle to pack.

Sunscreen is an absolute must! If you don't wear sunscreen when you're out all day in Kissimmee, you will get burned. Don't let a cloudy day fool you; you can still get badly sunburnt even when the sun isn't out! Sunscreen can be found at just about any store in

>TOURIST

and around Kissimmee, but make sure to buy it outside of the theme park areas or else it might be a lot more expensive.

Bug spray is also something you're going to need. While visiting Florida you'll meet some of your worst enemies: mosquitoes. These insects leave itchy bites that are hard to ignore, and they're all over the place, especially in the summer. If you plan on spending a lot of time outside, and especially if you'll be out at dawn and dusk, you'll need some bug spray to keep those mosquitoes away. Most stores around here will carry bug spray. Though the natural bug sprays might be a bit more expensive, I like to use those over the normal cheap sprays because they don't leave your skin gross and sticky.

If you don't have a good rain jacket, ponchos are available all over Kissimmee. They're usually pretty cheap, and can come with some cool designs! Once again, be sure to keep these with you always and buy them before you enter the theme parks, or else you might find yourself paying a lot more than you want to for a big piece of thin plastic. (Trust me, it's happened to me before!)

MONEY

6. WAYS TO PAY

Luckily, there are plenty of easy ways to pay in Kissimmee! Many places accept Apple Pay and Google Wallet now (they'll usually have a sign hanging up somewhere if they do), and just about everywhere takes credit/debit cards. Really the only places around Kissimmee that might not take cash are stalls at the farmer's markets. At Disney World, there's even another way to pay with MagicBands. If you're staying at a resort you will receive a MagicBand, which you have the option of linking up to your credit/debit card. Any purchases you make will be added to your room charge. All you need to do to make a purchase is scan the MagicBand at just about any Disney World location and enter your MagicBand PIN number. The MagicBand can also be used to pay when you purchase a Disney Dining Plan.

7. CASH

It's always good to have cash on you, just in case something malfunctions or you come across a rare place that only takes cash. Most establishments will take large bills, but it's better to carry your money in denominations of $20 or less.

Loose change isn't really necessary. If you acquire some coins you might be able to gather enough to buy something small or make an engraved smashed penny at Disney, but lots of stores and restaurants now have donation boxes or tip jars where you can dump your change. Consider donating your change instead of letting it jingle around in your pocket!

8. TIPS: WHO TAKES THEM, WHO DOESN'T?

If you're a U.S. native, you're most likely you're familiar with adding a tip to your bill at a restaurant. If not, don't worry; it's simple! It's customary to tip 10-15% of your bill if you're at a sit-down restaurant. If you have an exceptionally large party, most restaurants remind you on your receipt that a larger gratuity is expected. Some quick-service restaurants have started asking for tips as well, but unless you have a waiter serving you throughout your meal, these tips for fast food and other similar types of restaurants are optional.

Not everyone takes tips, however. The grocery store chain Publix, which has locations all over Florida, does not allow their employees to accept tips. Many employees who work inside the theme parks are also not allowed to take tips. If you receive exceptional service, please check! Tips are always appreciated. If you see a tip jar, even just some extra change helps if you enjoyed your experience at that place!

9. BE PREPARED TO PAY EXTRA

With Kissimmee being a tourist city, sometimes goods can be more expensive than what you'd find around the rest of Florida. Inside the theme parks, especially, you'll find prices marked up several dollars! This is why it's always advised to buy essential items outside of the parks and to bring your own water bottle. If you want to save a little money, you also might want to think about buying a few simple groceries and bringing a meal to the theme parks rather than paying for every meal and snack. A peanut butter and jelly sandwich is my favorite homemade park meal! Another plus is that you can eat your homemade food while waiting in line.

>TOURIST

Also, be sure to thoroughly research the activities you plan on participating in. When you buy a ticket to Universal Studios for a day, it will not allow you access to Halloween Horror Nights; in fact, you will get kicked out of the park early when the event starts! Tickets for Halloween Horror Nights are separate from the park tickets. You'll find this to be the same at most of the theme parks with their special events.

Several popular places in Kissimmee, theme parks included, will charge you for parking. This fee can be pretty expensive, so make sure to be prepared!

10. BANKS AND ATMS

One of the great things about Kissimmee is you will never have trouble finding an ATM! They're everywhere: all around the city, in the theme parks, and at the malls.

If you're traveling from inside the U.S., most of the major bank chains have locations in the area, with the main banks being SunTrust and Bank of America. However, if you bank with Wells Fargo, note that there's only one bank location in the city and it's on the east side, away from the theme parks. You might have to travel 15-20 minutes or so to get to a Wells

Fargo bank.

Travel

11. GETTING AROUND

You have lots of options when it comes to travel, but the locals mainly drive everywhere. While we do have local buses and our new SunRail trains, residents of Kissimmee find it most convenient just to take their cars wherever they're going. That being said, if you're able to, I highly suggest renting a car. This will allow you to easily explore some other nearby cities and give you more freedom with your schedule.

Florida doesn't have the best public transportation, but if you can't rent a car, no worries! Uber and Lyft are great options for travel, and will often be cheaper than getting a taxi. If you're heading north/northeast, the SunRail train is very cheap and stops at some of the other major cities in Central Florida. It's kept up pretty well and it's a really nice ride; I've thoroughly enjoyed myself every time I've ridden it! It doesn't run on weekends, so make sure to keep that in mind. There are local bus systems as well, with plenty of

>TOURIST

bus stops all over Kissimmee.

Also note that Disney has its own bus system, which only travels within the Walt Disney World Resort area. They also have their "Minnie Van" service that functions through Lyft but is also only available to travel on Disney property and to/from the Orlando International Airport. Sometimes the Disney bus routes can get confusing, so make sure you plan ahead of time to make sure your location has a bus going to your next location! For example, there are no buses to any of the theme parks from Disney Springs, but you can take a bus from any of the theme parks to Disney Springs. I said it was confusing! You can find help with this by searching online, calling, or looking on the My Disney Experience app, which I'll get into more later.

12. FROM THE AIRPORT TO THE HOTEL

There are lots of taxi, bus, and shuttle services available at the airport. Cars will be available to rent as well. If you're staying at a Disney hotel, they offer a free Magical Bus Express service which takes you from the airport to select resorts for free! Also, as mentioned earlier, Disney's "Minnie Van" service can take you from the airport to select Disney resorts for a fee. These services are not available for every Disney resort, so be sure to make your plans in advance.

13. HIGHWAYS AND TRAFFIC

Several major roads around Kissimmee are commonly known to Central Florida residents, which I already talked a little bit about earlier. That being said, there are normally several routes to get to where you're going, so your GPS is your best friend! The route with less traffic will almost always be the quickest, even if a route is listed as faster with lots of backed up traffic. Speaking as someone who's lived here for a while and knows how to get pretty much everywhere, I always check my GPS before I take a 20+ minute trip. You never know when there might be an accident on the main road that has traffic stopped!

That being said, Central Florida is notorious for its traffic, especially in the Orlando/Kissimmee area. Between the times of 7:00-9:00am and 3:30-7:00pm, the infamous highway Interstate 4 and the main

>TOURIST

Kissimmee road 192 can be congested with an hour or more of traffic! A great way to get around most of the traffic (though you might not be able to beat it altogether) is by using toll roads or back roads. When you GPS directions to a location, consider asking the GPS to guide you in a way that doesn't use highways if you're traveling during rush hour. Or you can try to avoid traveling during rush hour altogether, though that may not be possible some days. Just know that at some point, you will probably have to sit through some traffic.

14. TOLLS

Though it does cost money to travel on the toll roads, take them into consideration when traveling. They're a great alternative to I-4, where construction and traffic can slow you down. The toll roads have some nice scenery and can be a considerably faster way to travel!

Many Floridians, especially those from the Orlando area, have what's called a SunPass, which you can attach to your car so that tolls are virtually added to an online account you pay. This can be a really useful thing to have when you visit because the small sticker costs virtually nothing, you can avoid gathering quarters to pay the tolls, and you don't have to slow down when going through a toll station! A SunPass can be purchased online or in many convenience stores in Kissimmee.

The main two toll roads in the area are 429 and 417, which then branch out into the turnpikes and other major highways if you plan on traveling further away. Both of these toll roads will take you North, though 429 travels on the West side and 417 will take you on the East. Depending on where you're going, these toll roads may be the best way to travel. There's rarely bad traffic on them!

15. PARTY OF ONE

Traveling by yourself? No problem! There are lots of great activities for individuals to do in Kissimmee. Also, a nice perk at the theme parks is getting to use the single rider line! Some popular attractions have separate and faster lines for single riders.

It really goes without saying, but just be aware of your surroundings, especially at night. Like many tourist areas, Kissimmee isn't always safe for someone traveling alone. Generally, it's best not to travel or walk alone at night, especially around 192 in Kissimmee. This is not a "dangerous city" necessarily, but as always, taking precautions will not hurt. Take some time to figure out all your transportation ahead of time so you're never stuck somewhere. If you're a night owl, there are plenty of safe places to hang out in the evenings like Celebration, Disney Springs, or CityWalk.

FOOD

16. FOOD FOR ALL TASTES!

Kissimmee is home to all kinds of different people, which means that the city has a great diversity of culture. One of the areas where this shows the most is in our food! No matter what kind of food you're craving, even if it's a taste of home, you can probably find it somewhere close by.

If you're looking for your favorite chain restaurant, you can most likely find that in Kissimmee as well! Just traveling down 192 you'll see popular restaurants lining both sides of the street for miles. You'll also see some familiar places at CityWalk and Disney Springs.

Though I'll talk about some specific places to eat, these are by no means the only great restaurants around! I won't even really cover the food at the theme parks (because that's a whole other book), so ultimately just know that no matter where you are in Kissimmee, you'll find something good to eat!

17. BREAKFAST/BRUNCH

There are so many wonderful places to eat in Kissimmee that it's hard to know where to begin! One of my favorite places to get breakfast/brunch is downtown Celebration. Not only are there some great places to eat and relax, but it's a beautiful place to walk around with some coffee and hang out with family. Sweet Escapes is absolutely a treat, with wonderfully crafted breakfast sandwiches, bagels, and lots of baked goods to choose from. Just down the street is Market Street Diner, which serves all sorts of breakfast entrees like parfaits, omelets, and biscuits and gravy. Just across the road from the diner is a Starbucks with a beautiful outside seating area that many locals (including me) often take advantage of!

If you're bringing your family, you can look into one of Disney's character breakfasts held at different locations all over their property. At these special breakfasts, you get to experience not only tons of great food but also meetings with different Disney characters! Though it might be pretty expensive for breakfast, it's especially a great time for kids. Some of my favorite childhood memories are experiencing the Ohana character breakfast at the Polynesian Resort.

18. QUICK BITES

With all the hustle and bustle around Kissimmee, the area is filled with quick service and fast-food restaurants if you need to grab some lunch or dinner. Plenty of familiar fast-food restaurants surround the Disney area, as well as some unique ones!

If you've traveled pretty far to come to Florida, one restaurant you should definitely experience is 4 Rivers. If you ask a Florida native about this chain BBQ restaurant, 99 out of 100 times their eyes will light up! It's just grown in popularity over the past few years, and there are a few locations around the Kissimmee area. 4 Rivers serves amazing barbecue with tasty sides and fun desserts with a rustic atmosphere.

Kissimmee residents are really attached to our own "street food" in the form of food trucks! While this trend has started up all around Central Florida, Kissimmee has adopted it in full force. Just down 192, close to Disney, is the World Food Trucks area where a variety of food trucks are open every day from 11:00am to the early hours of the morning. You'll also find food trucks frequently in downtown Celebration and at farmer's markets in the area. These trucks boast all different kinds of food, including gourmet mac and cheese, crepes, and burgers.

19. DINNER

Top-notch dinner restaurants can be found all over Kissimmee. Whether you're looking for a nice sit-down place like Charley's Steakhouse or a more casual atmosphere like Ari's Sushi Bar, there's something for you and your family to enjoy.

Some restaurants in Kissimmee don't serve just dinner, but an entire experience! Kobe's Japanese Steakhouse is popular throughout the United States for the chefs who make a show of cooking the delectable food right in front of you. Medieval Times is like dinner and a theme park show all at once!

>TOURIST

Diners get to be spectators at a fun medieval show including knights, horses, and jousting. A few places, like El Tapatio and Avocado Mexican Grill, have entertainment in the form of live music. These two restaurants bring out live mariachi bands to serenade you while you're eating the tasty Mexican food.

When it comes to food in Kissimmee, I invite you to explore! You might just find your new favorite place to eat!

20. FARMER'S MARKETS

Central Florida is known for having a great farmer's market scene. At these markets, you'll find lots of unique food, produce, and a friendly atmosphere. You can find one-of-a-kind meals here, as well as fun snacks and homemade wares. There are several great markets in and around the Kissimmee area, and the ones I'm about to mention are only the beginning!

Firstly is the farmer's market in Kissimmee, which takes place every Sunday morning in downtown Celebration. While this market is rather small, there are still a decent amount of stalls to look at, and you can explore downtown while you're there.

Heading 45 minutes southwest there's a much bigger farmer's market in Lakeland on weekend mornings, usually featuring a couple local solo musicians. Occasionally, there will be an event going on in the nearby park as well! This market has lots of food, plants, and fun crafty items to discover.

About 30-40 minutes northeast in Orlando, there are several farmer's markets in the area. Check out Winter Park and Lake Eola to be sure, but also search around for more!

A 20-30 minute skip down the scenic toll road 429 will take you to a hidden gem of a farmer's market in downtown Winter Garden on Saturday mornings. This large farmer's market is very dog-friendly and has lots of unique food stalls! (There's also a wonderful coffee shop right on the corner of the market!) There's a huge produce market here as well.

All of these markets usually open early in the morning around 8:00-9:00, and I advise you to get to them early before stalls start selling out! If you make it there a little later, no worries; there's still plenty going on at these farmer's markets until they close in the afternoon!

DRINKS AND SNACKS

21. COFFEE

Besides the popular chains like Starbucks and Dunkin' Donuts, there are some great coffee shops in Kissimmee! Cafe Express is a favorite in the area, and it's most likely close to where you're staying if you're here for Disney! They not only have great coffee, but amazing Latin American, European, and American cuisine as well. Braz Coffee and Tea is another popular local place located in downtown Kissimmee, and just across the street is Buchito, a Cuban cafe. Susan's Courtside Cafe is also another great coffee shop/cafe in downtown Kissimmee. These little cafes all have a nice, relaxing atmosphere amid historic downtown.

If you're heading to Disney or Universal you'll definitely find Starbucks inside the parks, but in Disney, you'll also discover Joffrey's, another coffee chain that has some great specialty drinks.

22. TEA

If you're a tea lover like me, you're in luck! There's so much great tea to be discovered in Kissimmee! One of the best places for tea is Celebration Tea Room, located on 192 just outside of Celebration. This place isn't just a tea room, but a restaurant serving breakfast, lunch, and dinner. However, they have a huge tea menu, and they also have different kinds of high tea options available. Inside is a quiet, whimsical atmosphere. You might pay a little more than you usually would for meals, but everything this place serves is exquisite, and you won't regret coming here. It's my favorite restaurant in the area, hands down!

Diane's Creations and Tea Room is located in Downtown Kissimmee and it also has a wide selection of teas and some tasty food. Make sure to check their hours before you go, because they're a little different than most places.

Of course, Joffrey's at Disney also offers a nice selection of tea, including very good tea lattes! And if you happen to be going to Epcot, make sure to check out the Twinings store in the United Kingdom pavilion!

>TOURIST

23. FAMOUS SNACKS

Even apart from the theme parks, Kissimmee and the surrounding area is home to lots of famous snacks for you and your family to try! Here's a list of just a few of the best.

First up is Voodoo Donuts, located at CityWalk just outside of Universal Studios. This place has become globally famous for its crazy flavored donuts! They are amazing and worth every penny, but be prepared to wait for greatness! There's almost always a long line.

Next is Pineapple Dole Whip, served at the Walt Disney World Resort. If you're familiar at all with the Disney parks, you've probably heard of this renowned treat! Most people enjoy the vanilla and pineapple swirl ice cream the best, which is only served at the Polynesian Resort, the Magic Kingdom, and Disney Springs. The pineapple flavor by itself can be found at almost any Disney location now!

One of the most frequented snack places in Kissimmee is Krispy Kreme. When their "hot donuts" sign is on, you'll want to get in there quick! Not only does Krispy Kreme serve incredibly good and fresh American donuts, but the location closest to Disney allows you to actually view the donut production line!

Hot dogs are no longer just hot dogs in Kissimmee; they've now evolved into almost gourmet dishes with all sorts of different toppings! Willy's Wieners is a local diner famous for their hot dogs, as the name would suggest. B.B. Wolf's Sausage Co. located in Disney Springs is a stand serving top-notch hot dogs and sausages with both traditional and unique toppings.

A snack that's made it's way to Florida from the northern U.S., poutine has become quite a trend in Kissimmee. This delectable snack of french fries with gravy and cheese curds might make your stomach uneasy later on, but it's worth every bite! The Daily Poutine is another stand in Disney Springs solely dedicated to this snack and variations of it. Otherwise, you can find poutine at several restaurants in the area, usually burger joints and other similar restaurants.

24. BAKERIES

One of my favorite things to do on a weekend morning is to get some baked goods to eat for breakfast and find a nice quiet place to read. Kissimmee is home to several Spanish bakeries, such as La Hacienda located on 192. As I mentioned

>TOURIST

earlier, Sweet Escapes in downtown Celebration has a huge case of baked goods and wonderful sweets! There are numerous cupcakeries in the area, not the least of which is Sprinkles (located in Disney Springs), which features a Cupcake ATM!

Also worth a mention is my favorite bakery located in Lakeland, about 45 minutes away. While it may be a bit of a drive, the distance won't even be an issue once you taste Born and Bread's food. This little bakery is exceptional and is becoming well-known all over Central Florida. Here you'll find all sorts of breads, croissants, cookies, cakes; you name it! They're only open Saturday mornings and Wednesday evenings, so it'll take a special trip, but it's well worth it!

25. COCA-COLA STORE

There's a rather unique store located in Disney Springs that's fun for the whole family: the Coca-Cola store, with three stories of Coke related products and merchandise as well as a rooftop "bar" that offers sodas from around the world, adult beverages, floats, and more! This is a one-of-a-kind store that you won't find anywhere else in Florida. In fact, there are only three of them in the U.S.! If you've brought your kids, they even have an opportunity to meet the Coca-Cola polar bear!

Shopping

26. MALLS

There are two outlet malls located in and near Kissimmee. One is the Orlando Vineland Premium Outlets near Disney World, and the other is the Orlando International Premium Outlets just outside Universal Studios. They feature different stores, so make sure to check out both outlet malls! You'll also find food courts and assorted snacks at both malls, so you don't need to make an extra trip for food.

There are plenty of shopping malls located around Kissimmee, though they are a little further out in Orlando. The closest is the Mall at Millenia, a more upscale place with Ikea right next door, and the Florida Mall, which is massive and contains many favorite stores!

Needless to say, if you have a favorite place to shop, just do a quick search and you'll most likely find it nearby!

>TOURIST

27. DISNEY SPRINGS

This area was just redone in the past few years and it's now one of the most popular hangout spots in Kissimmee! It features a huge variety of shops both familiar and brand new. The atmosphere is beautiful, relaxing, and fun for the whole family! With stores like Vera Bradley, Under Armor, and Lego, there's something to please everybody.

On top of the incredible amount of shops, there are also several restaurants at Disney Springs, ranging from themed dining like T-Rex and Rainforest Cafe to quick service like Earl of Sandwich and Polite Pig. You'll also find bakeries, coffee shops, bars, and other fun places to grab a bite while shopping!

Disney Springs especially comes to life at night, when musicians perform all over the area and special events take place. It's a really fun area to take the family to, and you'll never find yourself bored! Best of all, it's absolutely free to park and enter!

28. CELEBRATION

Celebration is a small town within Kissimmee that's located right next door to Disney and the major highway I-4. The community is very green and well maintained, and it's the perfect place to get away from all the hustle and bustle around the theme parks.

Downtown Celebration features a small collection of unique shops that you can't find anywhere else. Many of these places have been there for years, and you'll find lots of nice boutique stores amidst the calm, sunny atmosphere by the lake.

29. TOURIST SHOPS

All down 192 you'll find large tourist shops; you'll know them by their giant signs advertising cheap goods! Most of these places have pretty decent prices and you can buy all sorts of things like t-shirts, beach towels, and souvenirs. As would be expected, there are lots of Disney items sold here. If you're looking for matching Disney t-shirts for your family, these shops are the best places to look! A tourist shop is also a good alternative for Walmart if you need to buy a last-minute item like a hat, sunglasses, or a water bottle before you hit the parks.

>TOURIST

30. GROCERY STORES/SUPERMARKETS

No matter what part of Kissimmee you're staying in, there's a store for your needs! Walmart locations are scattered throughout Kissimmee and are great if you need to pick up anything you forgot to pack at a cheap price; just be ready to meet with some crowds!

CVS and Walgreens locations are also around. They're good small stores if you need to buy just one or two things quickly, though they may be a bit more expensive.

Grocery stores like Publix and Aldi are throughout Kissimmee as well, with Publix offering lots of familiar brands at reasonable prices. Though Aldi's brands might not be well known, they offer good quality products at really great prices.

DISNEY

31. PLANNING A DISNEY VACATION

If you've come to Kissimmee for the sole purpose of going to Disney World, that's fantastic! While there's a whole separate book that could be written on how to do a Disney vacation properly, I, as a frequent Disney-goer, do have some insider tips on how to get the most out of your Disney trip.

The number one thing I'll stress about a Disney vacation is that planning ahead is a necessity. With the sheer amount of things to do just on Disney property itself, you'll need to figure out what's most important for you and your family to do. If you need help with your planning, Disney's got you covered! Disney travel agents are available to help you plan your vacation and inform you of deals like a vacation package and dining plan. Depending on what you want your trip to look like, booking through a Disney travel agent may actually come out cheaper than trying to plan the trip all on your own, and it takes much of the weight off your shoulders when everything is planned out in advance.

>TOURIST

If you are planning the trip yourself, save some time to search around and take advantage of the offers on tickets, hotels, food, and more that Disney has throughout the year. It's best to buy park tickets directly from Disney, no matter how tempting cheaper prices from third parties are. You'll see lots of ads for impossibly cheap theme park tickets around Kissimmee, but many times these are scams.

32. GET THE APP!

The My Disney Experience app is a must-have at the parks. Once you link up your park ticket to the app, you can book FastPasses—a way to skip long ride lines—up to 30 days in advance! The app also shows you current wait times for all rides, as well as showtimes, park hours, and basically anything you need to know while you're at Disney. You can even mobile order food at some locations!

The app also helps you out with transportation. It shows you the bus schedules all over Disney, which is extremely helpful when you're traveling around Disney property. Basically, this app is one of the most helpful things you can have while you're at Disney World.

33. DISNEY RESORTS

If your vacation is centered around Disney, it's a good idea to think about staying at a Disney resort. While some of the resorts are very extravagant, others are actually comparable to other hotels and resorts off of Disney property. When you stay at a Disney resort you also get added benefits like Extra Magic Hours—early or late entry into the parks—the dining plan, and access to top-notch resort facilities. Besides, it's just really convenient to be so close to the theme parks, and all Disney resorts provide quick and free transportation to anywhere you want to go on Disney property.

34. MUST-SEES AND MUST-DOS

Of course, every family will have their own agenda of what they want to do at Disney, but there are definitely some iconic things at the parks you'll want to take advantage of…

A picture in front of Cinderella's Castle in Magic Kingdom is a must, even if you take it with your own

>TOURIST

camera rather than Disney's Photopass photographers. This is a picture you'll cherish forever!

Visiting the World Showcase in Epcot is a great way to spend a good part of the day. This area takes you "around the world" to different countries and it's even better during the famous Food and Wine Festival in the Fall, where there are too many food stalls to count, featuring authentic food from all around the world.

For the nerds and geeks in the family, you can fly the Millennium Falcon in Galaxy's Edge. That's right, you heard me! While the new Star Wars-themed area in Hollywood Studios may be smaller compared to the rest of the park, it's a Star Wars fan's dream come true!

The whole family will enjoy exploring the bioluminescence of Pandora at night. The Pandora area in Animal Kingdom is impressive, but it's truly magical at night, where the entire area, including the ground, the plants, and everything else is illuminated in bright greens and blues.

35. BESIDES THE PARKS...

Even if you don't visit the parks at all, there are plenty of other activities available on Disney property! There are two water parks first of all: Blizzard Beach and Typhoon Lagoon. There are also two fun mini-golf courses on property and arcades at every major resort. Disney Springs offers free parking and entry and hosts several shops, restaurants, and events.

If you're looking for a quiet, low budget day, consider exploring the Magic Kingdom resorts by taking the monorail around the loop. Make sure to stop by Wilderness Lodge as well, which you can get to by a fun boat ride! Each of these resorts has a unique theme with its own shops and restaurants. They are free to enter, and there's much to explore.

OTHER ATTRACTIONS

36. BEACHES

Florida is world-famous for its beaches! There are many to choose from, though the closest and most famous beaches are going to be on the east coast.

Cocoa Beach and New Smyrna Beach are great for surfing, while Daytona Beach and St. Augustine are ideal for lounging around and exploring. All of the beaches can get really crowded, especially in the summertime. New Smyrna tends to be one of the quieter beaches, and the town itself contains lots of small boutique shops and unique restaurants.

The closest popular beach on the west coast is Clearwater, which also has a nice little city around it! Many of these beach towns also have some great shopping areas and restaurants right on the beach.

37. OTHER MAJOR THEME PARKS

Looking for some other theme parks besides Disney? You've come to the right place! Just about 20 minutes down the highway in Orlando is SeaWorld, a cross between a theme park and an aquarium/zoo. About the same distance away you'll find Universal Studios and Islands of Adventure, famous for The Wizarding World of Harry Potter and rollercoasters like The Hulk.

Over in Tampa, about an hour west down the highway, is Busch Gardens, a sister park to

SeaWorld. This theme park is more focused on thrill rides. And only 45 minutes away in Winter Haven sits Legoland, a fun, imaginative theme park geared towards kids.

38. NATURE

You'll notice plenty of green everywhere in Central Florida. There are several great, quiet places to get in touch with nature. Very close to Kissimmee are the Everglades, the famous giant wetlands in the middle of Florida. Check out tours and attractions around the Everglades online; there are many different options!

Central Florida is also home to several natural springs, like Wekiwa and Gemini. You might have to drive an hour or so to get to these, but in addition to the spring water that's cold year-round, you'll find beautiful parks and trails surrounding the springs where you can spend a nice day outside.

There are some not so quiet places to explore nature as well! Gatorland is a popular attraction in Orlando, mostly meant for kids, where you can interact with some of Florida's wildlife. Wild Florida is an exciting place in Kissimmee that also features

>TOURIST

wildlife and even has some thrills for the whole family, like zip-lining!

39. CONCERTS

No matter what time of the year you visit Kissimmee, there's bound to be a concert somewhere close by. First, check out the Disney park Epcot to see if any festivals are going on; during certain parts of the year, there are concerts every night, and they don't require an extra ticket after you enter the park!

Close by in Orlando is the Amway Center, which hosts huge concerts. In the other direction is the MidFlorida Credit Union Amphitheater near Tampa, where you'll also find big-name concerts. And don't discount the Dr. Phillips Center either, which is a beautiful indoor concert hall that hosts musicals, concerts, and all kinds of fun events in the middle of Downtown Orlando.

40. WATERPARKS

There are plenty of waterparks in the area to combat the intense Florida heat! In Kissimmee itself, you have the Disney water parks, Typhoon Lagoon and Blizzard Beach. Typhoon Lagoon is famous for its giant wave pool, while Blizzard Beach features a giant water slide! Both waterparks have several smaller slides and rides to enjoy, but there are also plenty of areas where you can simply lounge around and enjoy the sun.

H2O Live! is a brand new waterpark in Kissimmee that has received really great reviews. Nearby in Orlando are the other theme park waterparks, Aquatica and Volcano Bay. Each waterpark is unique in its own way, so make sure to check them out online to see which one will suit you and your family best. One of my favorite things that almost all of these waterparks have is a lazy river, where you float or relax in an intertube and let the river carry you along.

Also keep in mind that most of the resorts and hotels in the area have large pools, and some even have mini-water park types of areas that are available to staying guests!

UNIQUE EXPERIENCES

41. ESCAPE ROOMS

A growing trend in the U.S. that has just recently

>TOURIST

spread to Central Florida is escape rooms. There are some in Kissimmee as well as in Orlando and the surrounding areas. These challenges are fun for the whole family! Escape rooms allow you to have fun and use problem-solving skills to...well, escape a room! Each escape room facility is unique and has different kinds of rooms, so make sure to check them out before you come! Dare 2 Escape is located down the main road 192 in Kissimmee, and though the building may look small, the rooms are so detailed and well thought out that you won't even notice once you're inside. MindGames Escape Rooms is another venue located in Kissimmee in the Old Town area, also off of 192. There are plenty of other escape room locations in Orlando as well!

42. SILVER MOON DRIVE-IN THEATER

Though this location is actually located 45 minutes away in Lakeland, it's well worth it to travel here, especially if you've never experienced a drive-in theater. The whole area is outdoors, and the tickets are very cheap. The theater plays movies that are currently in theaters, and you get to sit in your car (or bring some lawn chairs to sit on) and watch on a giant screen! One of the best parts is that you can bring your own snacks, or buy some of the cheap concessions they have. Also check for double features, which the theater frequently offers. Do note that this is a late-night activity, as the movies are only shown once it's dark outside. However, this drive-in is very family-friendly, and they often show the newest children's movies!

43. DISNEY WILDERNESS NATURE PRESERVE

Fond of peace and quiet and getting in touch with nature? Though Kissimmee might be a bustling city, there are lots of beautiful places set apart where you can experience nature at its finest. Disney actually has a nature preserve in Kissimmee that's absolutely free (yes, you heard that right)! The Disney Wilderness Preserve is a conservation area at the tip of the Everglades that houses over 1,000 species of plants and animals and has a beautiful 3-mile walk. Not only is it a great way to get in touch with nature, but it's educational too, and even the kids will love seeing all the different wildlife here!

>TOURIST

44. OLD TOWN

If you're anywhere near Kissimmee, you can't miss Old Town! Just look for the tall, flashing, crazy looking slingshot ride and Ferris wheel, and you've found it! Old Town is a unique collection of shops, restaurants, and rides (with Fun Spot America just next door)! There are different events there every night, and they're open late, so be sure to check out what's going on while you're here!

45. DOWNTOWN KISSIMMEE

If you head east through Kissimmee you'll come to the historic downtown of the city, about 40 minutes away from Disney World. Downtown has some wonderful shops and unique restaurants that are mentioned throughout this book. There are also some great historical sites to check out! It's the perfect place to take a nice walk with your family and see some new things.

GET CULTURED

46. THE LANGUAGE

While almost every single native Kissimmee dweller will speak English, there are also a lot of Spanish speakers living in the city. In fact, Spanish is the second most spoken language in Florida. Due to this diversity in culture, many announcements and signs, especially at the theme parks, will be in both English and Spanish.

You'll most likely be able to find maps, instructions, and signs in your most comfortable language. The theme parks are filled with people who will be able to communicate with you and your family. Though we might speak English, we want you to have the best time possible here even if you don't!

47. WE'RE NEVER STRANGERS FOR LONG!

Around Kissimmee, if you're around a stranger for more than a minute or so, you're usually not a stranger after that minute. I can't tell you how many times I've struck up a great conversation with

>TOURIST

someone who lives on the other side of the world! If you do venture into the theme parks, or even restaurants and shops, feel free to interact with the employees and other tourists or natives you might meet. If you see someone wearing a t-shirt or hat you like, compliment them! You'll rarely ever get a frown in return.

48. BE KIND!

Most establishments in Kissimmee, from restaurants to hotels to theme parks, train their employees on how to interact with tourists. We love tourists here! Employees of all kinds interact with people from several countries every single day, and while a language or social barrier may be difficult to get through, please remember that they are people, and are (hopefully) doing their best to serve you! This tip really goes without saying, but it never hurts to emphasize how much it can make someone's day when you're just kind, even if you're stuck in an irritating situation.

49. ART AND MUSIC

Central Florida has a huge arts scene, featuring concerts, art festivals, and other events all throughout the year. You're sure to find music and art to suit your tastes and experiences that are fun for the whole family! Right next door in Orlando are several art festivals that often feature local live music as well. These festivals have great local music, art, and crafts. I really enjoy going to these to browse the stalls, listen to great music, and hang out with my family and friends. It's a really fun and relaxing atmosphere.

50. PLEASE RECYCLE AND CLEAN UP!

While the United States, and Florida especially, hasn't always been the best about recycling, there has been a huge push in recent years to get everyone to recycle! Not only does it help the environment as a whole, but it helps protect our native Florida wildlife and helps keep our beautiful beaches clean! Lots of establishments, including the theme parks and lots of hotels and restaurants, have plenty of recycling bins available for your convenience. If you don't see one near you, always ask before you throw away something you could be recycling!

Also, make sure to clean up after yourself as best you can. While it seems like this is just common sense, some people (both residents and tourists) leave their trash in public areas because they know there are custodians to clean up after them. Everyone, from employees to residents, to fellow tourists, will appreciate it when you leave a place as clean as you found it.

51. EXPLORE!

With so many things to do in Kissimmee, so much different food to try, and all sorts of fun to be had, my best advice when visiting the city is this: be brave. Step out of your comfort zone and explore the area! You'll never be disappointed at what you'll find. And most of all, have fun. Make memories. I hope you have a fantastic time in one of the best cities in the world!

>TOURIST

TOP REASONS TO BOOK THIS TRIP

1. The sheer amount of different activities and experiences available.

2. The location allows easy and quick access to several other great destinations.

3. Something enjoyable for every member of the family.

>TOURIST

OTHER RESOURCES:

https://www.experiencekissimmee.com

https://www.experiencekissimmee.com/visitor-information/maps-area-guide

https://www.visitflorida.com/en-us/cities/kissimmee.htm

https://www.tripadvisor.com/Attractions-g34352-Activities-Kissimmee_Florida.htm

https://disneyworld.disney.go.com/vacation-ideas

https://www.mousesavers.com/walt-disney-world-vacation-discounts-and-deals/step-by-step-guide-to-planning-a-disney-world-vacation

>TOURIST

PACKING AND PLANNING TIPS

A Week before Leaving

- Arrange for someone to take care of pets and water plants.
- Email and Print important Documents.
- Get Visa and vaccines if needed.
- Check for travel warnings.
- Stop mail and newspaper.
- Notify Credit Card companies where you are going.
- Passports and photo identification is up to date.
- Pay bills.
- Copy important items and download travel Apps.
- Start collecting small bills for tips.
- Have post office hold mail while you are away.
- Check weather for the week.
- Car inspected, oil is changed, and tires have the correct pressure.
- Check airline luggage restrictions.
- Download Apps needed for your trip.

Right Before Leaving

- Contact bank and credit cards to tell them your location.
- Clean out refrigerator.
- Empty garbage cans.
- Lock windows.
- Make sure you have the proper identification with you.
- Bring cash for tips.
- Remember travel documents.
- Lock door behind you.
- Remember wallet.
- Unplug items in house and pack chargers.
- Change your thermostat settings.
- Charge electronics, and prepare camera memory cards.

\>TOURIST

READ OTHER GREATER THAN A TOURIST BOOKS

Greater Than a Tourist- Geneva Switzerland: 50 Travel Tips from a Local by Amalia Kartika

Greater Than a Tourist- St. Croix US Birgin Islands USA: 50 Travel Tips from a Local by Tracy Birdsall

Greater Than a Tourist- San Juan Puerto Rico: 50 Travel Tips from a Local by Melissa Tait

Greater Than a Tourist – Lake George Area New York USA: 50 Travel Tips from a Local by Janine Hirschklau

Greater Than a Tourist – Monterey California United States: 50 Travel Tips from a Local by Katie Begley

Greater Than a Tourist – Chanai Crete Greece: 50 Travel Tips from a Local by Dimitra Papagrigoraki

Greater Than a Tourist – The Garden Route Western Cape Province South Africa: 50 Travel Tips from a Local by Li-Anne McGregor van Aardt

Greater Than a Tourist – Sevilla Andalusia Spain: 50 Travel Tips from a Local by Gabi Gazon

Children's Book: *Charlie the Cavalier Travels the World* by Lisa Rusczyk Ed. D.

> TOURIST

Follow us on Instagram for beautiful travel images:
http://Instagram.com/GreaterThanATourist

Follow *Greater Than a Tourist* on Amazon.
>Tourist Podcast
>T Website
>T Youtube
>T Facebook
>T TikTok
>T Goodreads
>T Amazon
>T Mailing List
>T Pinterest
>T Instagram
>T Twitter
>T SoundCloud
>T LinkedIn
>T Map

> TOURIST

At *Greater Than a Tourist*, we love to share travel tips with you. How did we do? What guidance do you have for how we can give you better advice for your next trip? Please send your feedback to GreaterThanaTourist@gmail.com as we continue to improve the series. We appreciate your constructive feedback. Thank you.

>TOURIST

METRIC CONVERSIONS

TEMPERATURE

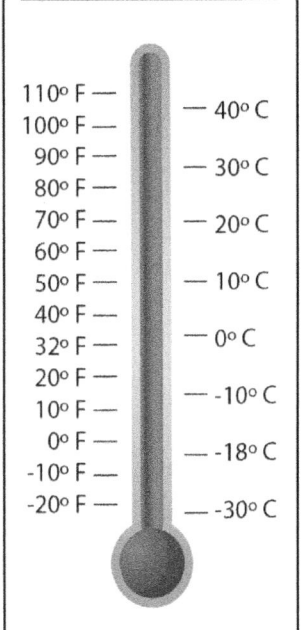

110° F — — 40° C
100° F —
90° F — — 30° C
80° F —
70° F — — 20° C
60° F —
50° F — — 10° C
40° F —
32° F — — 0° C
20° F —
10° F — — -10° C
0° F —
-10° F — — -18° C
-20° F — — -30° C

To convert F to C:

Subtract 32, and then multiply by 5/9 or .5555.

To Convert C to F:
Multiply by 1.8
and then add 32.

32F = 0C

LIQUID VOLUME

To Convert:................Multiply by
U.S. Gallons to Liters................. 3.8
U.S. Liters to Gallons 26
Imperial Gallons to U.S. Gallons 1.2
Imperial Gallons to Liters....... 4.55
Liters to Imperial Gallons 22
1 Liter = .26 U.S. Gallon
1 U.S. Gallon = 3.8 Liters

DISTANCE

To convert ....Multiply by
Inches to Centimeters 2.54
Centimeters to Inches 39
Feet to Meters...................... .3
Meters to Feet 3.28
Yards to Meters 91
Meters to Yards 1.09
Miles to Kilometers 1.61
Kilometers to Miles............ .62
1 Mile = 1.6 km
1 km = .62 Miles

WEIGHT

1 Ounce = .28 Grams
1 Pound = .4555 Kilograms
1 Gram = .04 Ounce
1 Kilogram = 2.2 Pounds

77

>TOURIST

TRAVEL QUESTIONS

- Do you bring presents home to family or friends after a vacation?
- Do you get motion sick?
- Do you have a favorite billboard?
- Do you know what to do if there is a flat tire?
- Do you like a sun roof open?
- Do you like to eat in the car?
- Do you like to wear sun glasses in the car?
- Do you like toppings on your ice cream?
- Do you use public bathrooms?
- Did you bring a cell phone and does it have power?
- Do you have a form of identification with you?
- Have you ever been pulled over by a cop?
- Have you ever given money to a stranger on a road trip?
- Have you ever taken a road trip with animals?
- Have you ever gone on a vacation alone?
- Have you ever run out of gas?

- If you could move to any place in the world, where would it be?

- If you could travel anywhere in the world, where would you travel?

- If you could travel in any vehicle, which one would it be?

- If you had three things to wish for from a magic genie, what would they be?

- If you have a driver's license, how many times did it take you to pass the test?

- What are you the most afraid of on vacation?

- What do you want to get away from the most when you are on vacation?

- What foods smell bad to you?

- What item do you bring on ever trip with you away from home?

- What makes you sleepy?

- What song would you love to hear on the radio when you're cruising on the highway?

- What travel job would you want the least?

- What will you miss most while you are away from home?

- What is something you always wanted to try?

>TOURIST

- What is the best road side attraction that you ever saw?
- What is the farthest distance you ever biked?
- What is the farthest distance you ever walked?
- What is the weirdest thing you needed to buy while on vacation?
- What is your favorite candy?
- What is your favorite color car?
- What is your favorite family vacation?
- What is your favorite food?
- What is your favorite gas station drink or food?
- What is your favorite license plate design?
- What is your favorite restaurant?
- What is your favorite smell?
- What is your favorite song?
- What is your favorite sound that nature makes?
- What is your favorite thing to bring home from a vacation?
- What is your favorite vacation with friends?
- What is your favorite way to relax?

- Where is the farthest place you ever traveled in a car?
- Where is the farthest place you ever went North, South, East and West?
- Where is your favorite place in the world?
- Who is your favorite singer?
- Who taught you how to drive?
- Who will you miss the most while you are away?
- Who if the first person you will contact when you get to your destination?
- Who brought you on your first vacation?
- Who likes to travel the most in your life?
- Would you rather be hot or cold?
- Would you rather drive above, below, or at the speed limited?
- Would you rather drive on a highway or a back road?
- Would you rather go on a train or a boat?
- Would you rather go to the beach or the woods?

>TOURIST

TRAVEL BUCKET LIST

1.

2.

3.

4.

5.

6.

7.

8.

9.

10.

>TOURIST

NOTES

Printed in Great Britain
by Amazon